I Identify

To The O'Coin Grandchildren,

You are strong,
You are kind,
You are loved!

♡ Sara K.

I Identify

Written by **Erin McCormack**
Illustrations by **Riky Audy**

I IDENTIFY

Copyright © Erin McCormack, 2023

All rights reserved. No part of this publication may be reproduced, stored in a retrieval system, or transmitted in any form or by any means, electronic, mechanical, photocopying, recording, or otherwise, without written permission of the author and publisher.

Illustrations by Riky Audy

Published by: McC Or Mack Books, Edmonton, Canada

ISBN 978-1-77354-501-1

www.iidentifybook.com

Publication assistance and digital printing in Canada by

PageMaster.ca

You are unconditionally loved
from your first breath until my last.

I identify as a child

I am the first born child to my mom and dad. I have extra responsibilities and take care of my siblings, but I get to stay up 30 minutes later than them and get mom and dad all to myself.

I identify as fast

When I race my friends at recess, I come in first every time. The class calls me The Flash and it makes me feel extra special.

I identify as strong

I wasn't always able to do it but now, I can cross the entire monkey bars both ways and not fall once.

I identify as brave

I used to be afraid of heights, but now I can climb almost any tree and see the world like a bird.

I identify as kind

My friend Holly spilled her soup, I ran to help her clean it up. She started to cry but I told her it's ok, we all have accidents sometimes and that made her smile.

I identify as generous

My mom packed me my most favourite snack, but my friend Morgan forgot his lunch so instead of just giving him my cucumbers I gave him half of my favourite snack.

I identify as funny

I like to pretend to fall down to make my friends laugh, I love seeing people laugh.

I identify as adventurous

I will always try new things; foods, sports, games, and experiences. Sometimes I am nervous or scared but after I try I am always proud of myself.

I identify as smart

I may find some work intimidating, but once I make myself understand then it becomes easy and I can help my friends understand too.

I identify as musical

I don't play any instruments, but I can listen to music and remember all the words to all the songs and I will sing them at the top of my lungs when I am all alone.

I identify as stylish

I have a style all my own. I like to wear bright colours and as many colours as I can put on. Sometimes my choice of clothes makes people smile, I like that colours makes people smile.

I identify as a child of God

I am who I am because God made me. He thought about every hair on my head. I am fearfully and wonderfully made by him on purpose for a purpose.

I identify as perfectly made and uniquely me

·:· Coming Soon! ·:·

The Woodchuck Woods

The Sparrow and the Raccoon

K eep an eye out for the new upcoming series called *The Woodchuck Woods*. This series entails stories of valuable lessons for children, and teaches adults how to approach teachable experiences with children.

The first book in *The Woodchuck Woods* series is *The Sparrow and The Raccoon*. Sparrow learns a valuable lesson about rumours and reputation and the power of our words. Follow the animals of The Woodchuck Woods as they experience real world situations and learn in a way where they are loved, forgiven, and accepted for the animal they are no matter their differences.

www.TheWoodchuckWoods.com

About the Author

Erin is a storyteller who loves to see the world through a child's eyes. Mother of two and always up for adventure, she loves to see children be supported in their strengths, encouraged to try new things, and be held accountable for their actions for the opportunity to learn and grow.

Born among the forests, lakes, and woodland creatures of Sudbury Ontario, then moving to the big skies and vast prairies of Alberta and meeting her forever soulmate, Erin believes life is an adventure and we just need to remember to slow down and look at the world again in wonder and awe just as we did as a child.